Contents

KU-213-720

SECTION 1 Home, Discreet Home   11

SPIES UNLIMITED

A secret stash of poems, jokes, riddles, and plots
uncovered by Andrew Fusek Peters

Illustrated by Bernice Lum

OXFORD
UNIVERSITY PRESS

OXFORD
UNIVERSITY PRESS

Great Clarendon Street, Oxford OX2 6DP

Oxford University Press is a department of the University of Oxford.
It furthers the University's objective of excellence in research, scholarship,
and education by publishing worldwide in

Oxford New York

Auckland   Cape Town   Dar es Salaam   Hong Kong   Karachi
Kuala Lumpur   Madrid   Melbourne   Mexico City   Nairobi
New Delhi   Shanghai   Taipei   Toronto

With offices in

Argentina   Austria   Brazil   Chile   Czech Republic   France   Greece
Guatemala   Hungary   Italy   Japan Poland   Portugal   Singapore
South Korea   Switzerland   Thailand   Turkey   Ukraine   Vietnam

Oxford is a registered trade mark of Oxford University Press
in the UK and in certain other countries

British Library Cataloguing in Publication Data

Data available

ISBN-13: 978-0-19-276331-0
ISBN-10: 0-19-276331-8

1 3 5 7 9 10 8 6 4 2

Printed in Great Britain by Cox and Wyman Ltd,
Reading, Berkshire.

SECTION 2 School

SECTION 3
The Explosive, Action-packed Finale 87

SECTION 1
Home, Discreet Home

This Introduction Will Self-destruct in Thirty Seconds

Welcome to my secret book.
Should I let you take a look?
If you break the hidden codes,
It might be that this book explodes!
Will you risk it? Will you try?
Do you want to be a spy?
Stories, riddles, gadgets galore,
Turn the page to find out more!

I'm a Spy, Get Me Out of Here!

It all began when I was three,
Began to question my family . . .
Most little boys want to know
'Why are clouds grey? Where does the wind blow?'
But I asked my mother, the one I adore
'Tell me, who are you working for?'
Soon, as part of my cunning plan,
I'd interrogated my Action Man,
Taken apart the garden mower
And built a remote-control flame-thrower.
I learned to read from an early age,
Devouring code books page by page.
Most boys make noise, I didn't do that
But learnt to stalk as quiet as a cat,
Surprise my parents—and that is why
When I grow up, I'm going to be a SPY.

Cast of Characters

Dad likes to think that he's a spy
(I also believe that sausages fly!).

Mum tries too hard, as you can see,
She hasn't got a clue about secrecy.

Here we have my baby bro,
He works under-the-cover
(you don't want to know).

Meet my sister, goes by the name of Dot.
Could she be an agent? I think not!

That only leaves my best mate Stan—
When it comes to sleuthing, he's the man!

George – Dangerous and Deadly!

With my black belt in karate
I quell my foes with a stare!
I am the stalking tiger,
With a spring I leap through the air . . .

My body is a killing machine,
A flick of my finger, you're dead!
Mum shouts out from downstairs:

'Hey, **wake up,
sleepy head!'**

Wannabe Spies

My mum and dad both wanna be
The best spies in this family.
Oh, if only they could see,
In spying tests, they'd get an Ɛ,
Always following me around,
Pretending not to make a sound . . .
How can I invite my friends for tea?
Ɛmbarrassment! It's killing me!

Uncoded Message

The door slammed open
And the woman ran in at a crouch,
Then swept her hand over the walls.
'Good! No listening devices!' she said to her wristwatch.
She looked under the light, peered into sockets,
Shook my Playstation, peered out of the window
And checked the bed.
'Clear!'
By now she was getting close to my bed
Until suddenly, her face was looming over me.
I was terrified.
'Right! I have one message to pass on. It's an
    important one.
Your whole future rests on how you respond!
Get it wrong and there will be trouble!'
I am in no doubt of that fact.
'I'll only say it once.

After speaking, it's possible my patience will self-destruct!'
I wonder what she'll say?
Maybe the world is at risk and they need me,
George Junior,
To leap in and save the day!
She opens her mouth one more time and I'm ready
To spy for my country,
To use impossibly groovy gadgets,
And fight really bad baddies.
But the message, once I manage to decode what
Falls from my Mum's frothing mouth, is:

'TIDY YOUR ROOM!

NOW!'

My parents are very odd sometimes...

My Dad

My dad has no fashion sense.
He wears dark glasses (in the dark)
And a long, beige raincoat (in the living room)
He has tinted all the windows in his car, which means
He is always driving into lamp-posts.

My dad is dead embarrassing.
All the way to school, he hops, scuttles, and jumps
From doorway to shadow,
To crouching position behind bus-shelters.
I try to walk five yards in front of him at all times.

My dad is disgusting.
I keep seeing him sticking his hands
In public rubbish bins and rootling among
The rotten food.
How can he do this to me?

My dad is definitely a bit odd.
He likes to whisper into his shirt lapel.
He picks up the phone, then puts it down,
Then picks it up, looks out of the window (carefully)
And puts it down again.

When a friend of mine comes round for tea,
(This happens less and less these days!)
My dad sticks a spotlight in their face
And asks my friend's name over and over again
And asks why he's come to our house,
And who is he working for.
My dad needs help.

Watch Out For George!

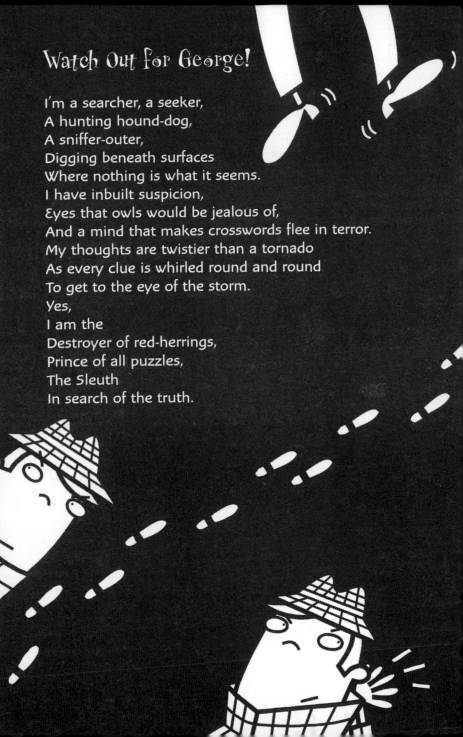

I'm a searcher, a seeker,
A hunting hound-dog,
A sniffer-outer,
Digging beneath surfaces
Where nothing is what it seems.
I have inbuilt suspicion,
Eyes that owls would be jealous of,
And a mind that makes crosswords flee in terror.
My thoughts are twistier than a tornado
As every clue is whirled round and round
To get to the eye of the storm.
Yes,
I am the
Destroyer of red-herrings,
Prince of all puzzles,
The Sleuth
In search of the truth.

Curiosity

There is an old saying that goes,
Curiosity killed the cat.
Sniffing around with his nose,
Now he's dead. How dumb is that?

That feline was stupid and slow
And suffered for being dozy;
To be a spy, it pays to know
You have to be quick and nosy.

Diary of a Spy

Monday:
Make a list of potential suspects and dodgy premises. Everyone has something to hide.

Tuesday:
I have **bin** following the rubbish men all day. Am on to their disgusting schemes and **refuse** to give up.

Wednesday:
Observe fish & chip shop. Something **cod** going on in that **plaice**.

Thursday:
Steak out the butcher's. A perfect **meating** place.

Friday: All those people going in and out of the veg shop, it's **extra-strawberry**. Need to **orange** better surveillance.

Saturday:
The plumber—must **tap** her phone. Spy-work is really **drain**ing

Sunday:
Suspect I'm coming down with a cold. Watch the box (very closely).

Favourite Spy Books

A Midsummer Night's Secret Mission

Alice in Undercover Land

Alice Through the Two-Way Looking Glass

Tom's Midnight Garden Meeting Place

The Big Friendly Agent

James and the Agent Peach

DANNY, THE CHAMPION SPY OF THE WORLD

Double-Agent Act

Harry Potter and the Chamber of Secrets

Oh, Crumbs! My Time is Up!

I spy with my little eye,
It's time for Mr Bread to die.
How did I end his floury life?
I simply used a kitchen knife.
I know that it was not so nice,
But Mr Bread is now a slice.
I don't mean to brag or boast,
But Mr Bread is dead! He's toast!

Of course, our house makes the perfect training ground for a spy: let me explain ...

The Traitor Within

I am stalking around with breath bated
For our house has been infiltrated
By a baddie who has to be caught,
The only description—'he's short.'
But now, I have picked up his tail,
And can tell that it's him by his wail.
But beware, for this monster can fell
A human just simply by smell.
I warn you that you won't live long
When exposed to the horrible pong.
Have you guessed yet that this enemy
Is somehow related to me?
This spy admits he's defeated,
And it's time that our hero retreated
To summon the troops (it's that bad!),
We must call upon our mum and dad.
The enemy smiles. Does he care
As a terrible stench fills the air?
The grown-ups look pale and unhappy
At this bomb that explodes from the nappy!

You don't have to be a spy to work out who made that smell!

27

I Spy

I spied my mum and dad having an argument.
It began with the usual
Undercover glances
And not-so-secret hand gestures.

I spied my mum and dad having an argument.
I took cover when the sniping started,
Hid my head under an armoured pillow.

I spied my mum and dad having an argument.
Sharp whizzing words rat-a-tatted from their mouths.
This was all-out war!

I spied my mum and dad having an argument,
Decided to blow my cover and blow my top.

'STOP!'
I cried
And they looked shocked and sheepish.

I stopped my mum and dad having an argument,
It took hours of interrogation.
But finally, under the spotlight,
They admitted they were wrong!

Later (it's really no fun, admitting this),
I spied them having a yucky kiss!

For my birthday, I got the best gift ever from Uncle Quentin!

Nano-spring Socks

When you get given socks,
It's hard but you must smile,
Put on your best behaviour
And go the extra mile.

Why do grown-ups do this?
It's torturously cruel,
But worse for us poor kids:
Such gifts are so uncool.

Unless it's Uncle Quentin
('Call me Q for short')
Whose gifts are guaranteed
To be quite a different sort.

For instance, there's his socks
That have been known to trounce
The enemy who's chasing you;
For just you watch them bounce!

With hidden nano-springs
And computer-aided flight,
Just take a step and say goodbye
And **WHOOSH!** you're out of sight.

This sock-it, rocket to 'em
Is made with attitude,
And if you own a pair
You are one lucky dude!

The Case of the Missing Sock

When the washing is finally dry,
The result is enough to make you cry.
The whole of the family goes into shock
As there's always at least one missing sock.
Now, normally I wouldn't care
If they vanished into thin air;

Socks are dull, they are no fun
But this time it's my favourite one!
It's time that this came to a stop—
I can no longer leap, but hop!
So, I say, enough is enough,
I'll get the thief who's nicked this stuff!

WHERE'S my nano-spring sock?

Action Stations

I crawled inside the washing machine,
Me and my camera at the foul crime scene.
(Don't do this at home.)
I dusted around for fingerprints,
(Including a pair of my underpants—yeuchhh!)
Took out my magnifying glass
To check out fluff and study dust
(And found a bit of last-week's pizza behind
The laundry basket—oh, yummy. And it had fur on it.)
I interviewed the family, who admitted,
This act had all of them outwitted.
Should I believe them? Hmmm . . .
Nothing, zilcho, not a sausage or a bean.
Though I wonder about that washing machine . . .

No luck so far. I'll just have to borrow my sister's tracking device.

Follow That Trail!

Give a tweak,
Twist the head,
Beep beep beep,
Straight ahead.

Feel revolted,
Comb those hairs,
Homing beacon
Says downstairs.

Oh so close now,
I can't miss—
But interrupted
By my sis!

She sees it all,
My face goes red.
A Barbie doll!
I wish I was dead!

35

As it was my sister's doll, I had to let her help me. The trail led down into the cellar... and guess what we found?

Acrostic Riddle

So there we were, deep
Underground,
Really dark
Prowling around.
Right! We're close now
I can see!
Surrender,
Evil thief, to me!

George and Stan's
Getaway Plan

Right, set state-of-the-art alarm system in case
of baby bro-incursion!
(Empty crisp packets placed by door.)

CHECK.

CD of typical-thumping-round-the-room-boy-noises.

CHECK.

High-wattage spotlight set up with cut-out
silhouettes-in-window in case passers-by
should look up from street (bedside lamp
and manky bits of cardboard).

CHECK.

High-tensile-super-strength-nylon-alloy-fibre
to abseil out of window (dad's old towing rope).

CHECK..

Check coast is clear of parent-patrols
with infra-red-night-sight-goggles
(grandma's old specs).

CHECK.

CHECK check shirt.

What?

Nothing, I just want to check I'm wearing my new
check shirt. Dad got it.

Right.

All systems go. Roger and out.

Who's Roger?

Oh, never mind.

Who Does He Think He Is?

Peeking in people's windows,
Kn**O**cking on doors when no one is in,
Peering through letterboxe**S**,
Dropping off s**t**range parcels,
Running **m**adly away from dogs,
Using a uniform **a**s a disguise.
Nope. He does**n**'t fool us for one second.

Spy-ku

Autumn in the park:
The intrepid duo spy
Leaves falling from trees.

It's Not Safe Out There

Spies in the kitchen,
Spies behind the door,
Spies in the cupboard,
And under the floor.

Spies on the TV,
Spies in space,
Spies in the park,
All over the place.

Spies have infiltrated,
They're hard to avoid,
I know they're out to get
Poor **Peter Aranoid**.

Who Said Going Undercover Was Fun?

when
i
pre
-tend
to
be
a
tree
it
helps
that
i
am
quite
skin-
ny
but
then
what
ru-
ined
my
dis-
guise
was
that
dog-
gy's
wet
sur-
prise!

SECTION 2
School

In front of 200 pupils, assorted teachers and an
Ofsted inspector...

Assembly

'What will you be, when you grow up?'
Said the Head. 'When you're a man?'
As he patted my head annoyingly
As only a grown-up can.

'I want to be a spy!' I said,
'With special X-ray eyes,
To uncover double agents,
Expose their cunning lies!'

'You want to be a spy?' he sighed.
'Oh my, that will be fun!
What can you see, when you study me?'
'I spy your fly's undone!'

Double Trouble

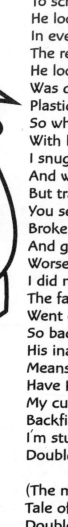

Sent my double
To school today.
He looked like me
In every way.
The reason that
He looked like me
Was due to
Plastic surgery.
So while he struggled
With literacy
I snuggled in bed
And watched TV.
But tragedy struck;
You see, my double
Broke the rules
And got in trouble.
Worse than this,
I did not like
The fact my double
Went on strike.
So back at school,
His inattention
Means that I
Have HIS detention!
My cunning plan
Backfired on me,
I'm stuck with
Double History . . .

(The moral of this
Tale of woe:
Double trouble is a
NO-NO!)

Some guy was passing a message round the class-room. By the time it got to me, I had no idea what he was on about!

Chinese Whispers

I really fancy Melissa.
Pass the message on.
From Jake Thackery.

I really fancy messing about.
Pass the mistletoe.
From Jane Thatcher.

Real fans mess up trout.
Parcel Mister Toe.
From Jammy Teacher.

psssst
psssst
psssst
psssst
Dead Dan's Mister
Nowt. Pass me my toast.
From a jogging creature.
Read,
Dan miss me out.
Pass me my toe.
From a jolly
teacher.
psssst
psssst

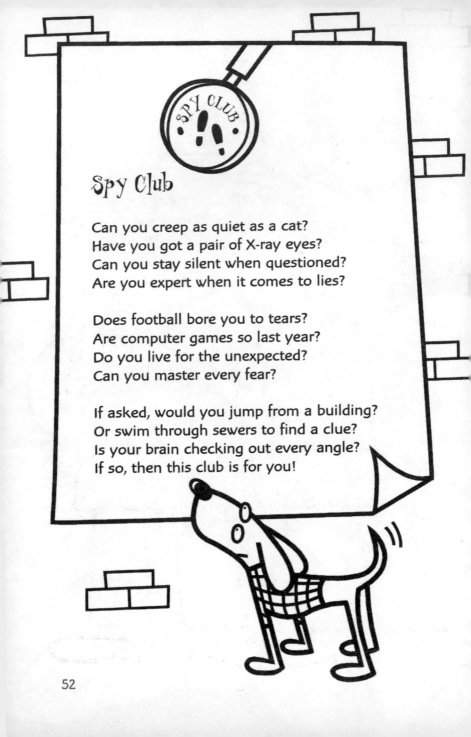

Spy Club

Can you creep as quiet as a cat?
Have you got a pair of X-ray eyes?
Can you stay silent when questioned?
Are you expert when it comes to lies?

Does football bore you to tears?
Are computer games so last year?
Do you live for the unexpected?
Can you master every fear?

If asked, would you jump from a building?
Or swim through sewers to find a clue?
Is your brain checking out every angle?
If so, then this club is for you!

53

Code Words

There're plenty of well-known code words
That existed in history
Like Abracadabra! Shazam!
And Open Sesame!

But in lots of books about spies
The passwords are somewhat stranger:
The Eagle Has Flown the Roost;
The Chicken of the East is Free-Range.

But these phrases are so weird,
The answer seems to me,
That spies should have their own
De-coding dictionary.

Spy Club – The Secret Language of Spies

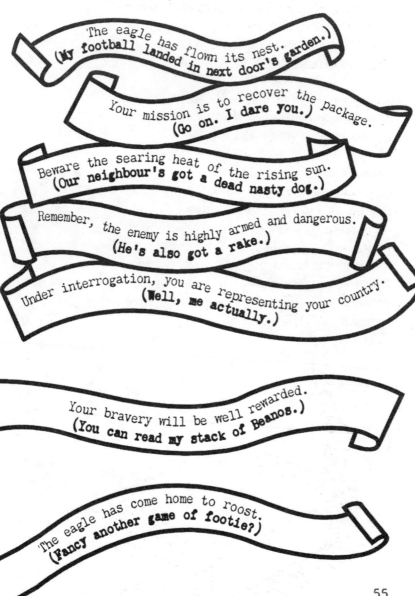

The eagle has flown its nest.
(My football landed in next door's garden.)

Your mission is to recover the package.
(Go on. I dare you.)

Beware the searing heat of the rising sun.
(Our neighbour's got a dead nasty dog.)

Remember, the enemy is highly armed and dangerous.
(He's also got a rake.)

Under interrogation, you are representing your country.
(Well, me actually.)

Your bravery will be well rewarded.
(You can read my stack of Beanos.)

The eagle has come home to roost.
(Fancy another game of footie?)

Here's one of the first missions we set prospective members!

Mission Chips

You will leave this room directly,
Take a left and walk one hundred metres.
At this point, bear right ninety degrees
And duck through the double doors.
Use the queue as cover. While you shuffle forward,
Try not to draw attention to yourself.
Remember!
You are acting as an ordinary child in an ordinary school
Having an ordinary, boring day.

Your contact will be standing in an apron.
When she raises a huge ladle in her left hand,
This will be your signal!
You will say, 'Chips and beans and pizza.'
She will say, 'I'm waiting.'

You will say, 'What?'
She will say, 'You heard me!'
You will say, 'Oh, all right then—**PLEASE!**'

You will grumble.
She will say, 'Anything else?'
You will say, 'No.'
She will say, 'No . . . what?'
You will say, 'No what what?'
She will go red in the face and repeat her code word
'No . . . what?'
You will say, 'I don't know Watt. Is he another pupil?'
Steam will issue from her ears and her head will begin
    the countdown to explosion.
This is your cue, Agent Dull!
You will immediately spin round
And deliver this important message:
'No, thank you!'
She will smile. The lives of innocent children will be saved.
Mission accomplished.

Naturally, we train our Spy Club members to be suspicious of everyone!

Top Five Evil Agents Infiltrating Our School

1 If I were you, I'd take a second look
At your so-called smiling cook.
At lunch, that innocent glop on the plate
Once eaten, might just seal your fate

2 Beware the secretary's wiles,
Her fingers hold a million files.
Believe me when I say she knows
Every time you blow your nose.
(You can never hide the spot
Where you rubbed that piece of snot!)

3   Her identity card calls her a nurse,
    But when uncovered, the truth is worse . . .
    When she promises that it won't hurt
    Don't be surprised when you hit the dirt!

4   They've got you sussed and know the facts
    As they whisper into their day-glo macs.
    The cars they stop are really annoyed,
    But the pupils should be paranoid!

5   Beware the dreadful eye that lingers,
    Beware the pointing of those fingers,
    Make a wish that you had fled,
    Before the summons of the Head.

We love our
Spy Club Magazine!

Spy Club Magazine

SPY CLUB

MATHS

I'm Going Crackers, Cracking Codes!

Codes are great fun. The first two are number codes. Each number matches up with a letter from the alphabet. See if you can work them out in your head.

Code:
1A 2B 3C 4D 5E 6F 7G 8H 9I 10J 11K 12L
13M 14N 15O 16P 17Q 18R 19S 20T 21U
22V 23W 24X 25Y 26Z

1. Fun
8 5 12 12 15

2. Fiddly
13 9 18 18 15 18 / 13 9 18 18 15 18 / 15 14 /
20 8 5 / 23 1 12 12
23 8 15 / 9 19 / 20 8 5 / 3 12 5 22 5 18 5 19 20 /
15 6 / 20 8 5 13/ 1 12 12?

Fantasy Lessons

3. Fiendish

2000 years ago, when Caesar needed to send secret battle plans to his generals he devised his own code.

Clue: for each letter, move back by three letters in the alphabet and see if it makes sense!

L / FDPH / L / VDZ / L / FRQTXHUHG / WKH / FRGH !

Answers on page 126!

Spy Club Magazine

ENGLISH

Love Sonnet to the Gadget of My Dreams

Shall I compare you to a summer's day?
You are more dinky and reliable.
Rough winds forever spoil my outside play—
This summer is not so desirable.
It hits the spot the way your features shine:
Your screen lights up when all the room is dimmed.
The price was fair, your functions mighty fine,
Your lightweight aluminium buttons trimmed.
Your eternal appeal will never fade;
As I possess you now, you are the best,
Putting other dead-dull gadgets in the shade
Thanks to the host of extras with which you're blessed.
So long as all those boys at school can see
That this is mine, so long lives wicked Jealousy!

Fantasy Lessons

The Princess Laments—a Limerick

There's a spy of whom I was fond,
Between us there was such a Bond.
I gave him a snog,
He turned into a frog:
That spy who was known as James Pond.

The Noun with No Name

It was a dark and gloomy paragraph.
We followed the
Verb without a Clause
Through
A
Long
Dark
Winding
Sentence,
Until
At
Last,
We
Came
To
A
Full
Stop
.
He
Had
Gone . . .
Leaving
Only an Exclamation Mark!

Work Out the Code

In this poem you have to work out what the
code word (sausages) stands for.
There are three levels of difficulty:

1. I went down to the **sausages** to buy some sausages.

2. We are developing super top secret **sausages**.
If you hit the intended target,
Everyone within a forty-five metre radius
Will be turned into sausages.

3. Sausages, sausages sausages in
The **sausages** twice, with **sausages**
Code red **sausages** to be **sausages**
Or not to be **sausages** that is the **sausages**!

If you decipher number three, you are a better
sausage than me. In fact you are one hot dog.
I will have to work hard to ketchup with you.

It's all
sausages
to me!

Spy Club Magazine

PE

Exercise Routine

I'm a
Traffic-swerving,
Alley-sprinting,
Garden-vaulting,
Rooftop-leaping,
Airplane-jumping,
Speedy-swimming,
Shark-avoiding,
Baddie-catching
Spy!

66

Fantasy Lessons

DRAMA

How to Act

To be or not to be who you are . . .
Work it out and you'll go far.
It takes cunning, ruthless tact
But we'll soon teach you how to act.
Spies who get in on this game
Win the opposite of fame.
With simple props, you've disappeared
Behind our combo wig-and-beard.
Save the country, earn applause
With a face that isn't yours.

Spy Club Magazine

GEOGRAPHY

A Riddle

Who is the most evil of them all?
Who is intent on world domination?
Who has the most cunning plan
Without exaggeration?

Who is the baddest baddy?
The prince of this perilous plan?
Have a guess, that this mess
Was the work of none other than . . . man.

Fantasy Lessons

Adverts for Spy Gadgets

WRITE SECRET MESSAGES, THEN EAT THE EVIDENCE!

THE SLICED LOAF NOTE PAD

A car that drives up walls

An inflatable motorbike

Someone's blown it up!

SUPER-SPIT

SUPER-SPIT

TRY OUR NEW SUPER-SPIT, GUARANTEED FRESH AND WILL LAST UP TO TWELVE MONTHS.

Lonely Hearts

Clapped out Cold-War Warrior
Seeks Official Secrets Act Secretary.
Please contact me by placing letter in bin at corner
Of Bond Street and Moneypenny Lane.

Would-be spyette,
Likes eating spy-getti
And watching **I'm a Spy, Get Me Out of Here**,
Seeks agent
For secret snogging sessions.

There is Something Wrong with Our Drama Teacher

Our teacher thinks he is so cool,
Acts as if he owns the school.
His shoes are made of crocodile skin
And what's the point of a platinum bin?
His mobile phone is solid gold,
He dyes his hair (but still looks old),
On his desk, a plasma screen.
No longer visits our canteen,
But has a chef for every whim.
He's given to airs! It's not like him.
His car? A red Ferrari Modena
With an in-built vacuum cleaner.
All this stuff must cost a packet,
Resulting from some dodgy racket.
Teachers weep at what they earn,
But this guy's got some dosh to burn!
Maybe pupil George can find out why . . .
It's time to play the part of SPY!

Wanted!

Have you seen this little old woman?
If you have, then tell us quick,
Ring this number: nine nine nine
And watch out for her walking stick.

She may look cute and ever so frail
But, as police, it's our belief
That underneath her wrinkled face
There lurks a ruthless, brutal thief.

If you catch her (are you bonkers?)
All the banks will be so jolly
And they'll give you your reward,
Ten per cent of all that lolly!

How to Follow a Suspect

We followed him down the street,
He didn't seem to care,
Our footsteps were fast and fleet
We travelled as quiet as air.

He didn't seem to care
But where was he going? we thought,
As we travelled as quiet as air
And hoped that he would be caught.

But where was he going? we thought,
Our teacher was up to no good.
And we hoped that he would be caught
So we tiptoed as best as we could.

Our teacher was up to no good
But he didn't seem to care,
So we tiptoed as best as we could
And travelled as quiet as air.

What kind of shoes does a spy wear?

HA! HA!

Sneakers

ssshhhhh!

The trail led us somewhere unexpected (and smelly).
We waited outside and watched to see what
would happen.

A Disgusting Transformation

Into the loo, there went a man,
Flushed his old face down the pan,
A little old lady came out of the loo.
Now Number One was Number Two.

The Plot Thickens (a Haiku)

Lady enters bank
Summer is a fruitful time
She comes out loaded.

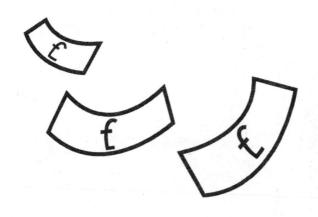

Time to Set the Trap

Give us the latest,
Get with it,
Foil your foe,
With Super Spit

Chew it up,
And open gob,
Finally give it
A straight lob.

As you watch
Saliva spin,
See it stretch out
Strong and thin.

With Super Spit
There is no hope
As enemies
Get tied by rope.

Baddies won't
Get away with it,
Thanks to our patented
Super Spit!

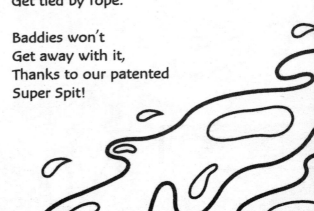

The Daily Messenger

FOUL FIEND FOUND!

The thief who robbed countless banks has been appre-hended.

DIABOLICAL DEEDS DISGUISED

The mysterious old lady was merely a disguise. The suspect wore a wig.

TERRIBLE TALE TIED UP!

Police were puzzled as they came upon the thief tied up with an advanced form of chewing gum.

DARING DRAMA DECEPTION

When the wig was removed, the suspect was found to be none other than the Drama Teacher of St Fleming School.

HUMBLE HEROES HAILED!

The identities of the brave duo who tackled this dangerous burglar are two pupils from the school, George Goldfinger and Stan Hidemore.

It's a Hard Life!

George and his mate Stan
Pulled off a cunning plan.
Brave, barmy, they were bold,
Grabbed the glory, got the gold.
What next? Suddenly
The whole' school's into secrecy.
No, it's not a surprise
Their club's full of spies.
Guess how the poem ends?
George, Stan, and loads of friends.

SECTION 3
The Explosive, Action-packed Finale

How to Detect a School Bully

Here are some clues:

1 He's in a gang (stupidity always congregates).

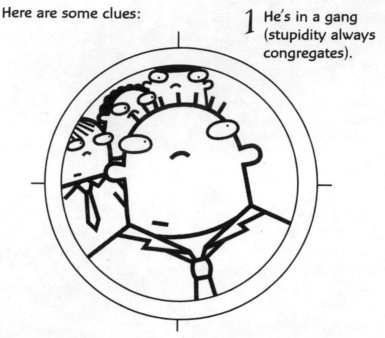

2 The insults themselves are always brain dead.

3 The smile on his face is sharp enough to cut down confidence.

4 He's guaranteed to be so thick a plank would be jealous and a brick could claim to be a long-lost cousin.

5 He likes to hang out in blind spots behind the loos and it's not just to say hello.

6 The way he clench-es his fists is not part of an exercise routine.

7 He thinks that bruises are a work of art.

8 His ability to create instant, indoor water-features (fea-turing fresh, flow-ing tears) is leg-endary.

Another Riddle

Answer on page 126!

My first is in flee, but not in run,
My second in wordplay, not in pun.
My third in old but not in dead,
My fourth in cool but not street-cred.
My fifth in toast but not in slice,
My sixth in water, never ice.
Put them together, it's what I do,
Just hope I don't come after you!

A Serious Case of Follow-itis

You are suffering follow-itis,
Your rash of questions is bad,
And if you are hearing alarm bells,
Then prying has made you mad!

To cure your snoopaholism,
This prescription might work, let's see.
Something dull to calm you down?
A daily dose of TV!

One afternoon Stan and I saw something suspicious going on ...

A Dodgy Deal?

George: Hey, check it out, take a look.

Stan: Isn't that Panz, our old school cook?

George: And who's he with . . . that's the Deputy Prime Minister.

Stan: (excited) I'm sure they're up to something sinister.

Deputy PM: Have you got what I asked for? I'm running late!

Panz: Don't worry. They're done. Keep your hair on, mate! Now listen! A deal's a deal. Pies for cash!

Deputy PM: Yes, yes. Don't breathe a word. Must dash!

George: I don't like the look of this lot.

Stan: They must be cooking up an evil plot!

Let me read what it says on the wrapper...

Panz's Perfect Porky Pies

Our ingredients are out of sight,
The taste will leave you in delight!
Open the wrapper, that fresh-baked smell
Will put you into a total spell.
Panz's Perfect Porky Pies
Are guaranteed to hypnotize!
The effect will leave you wanting more,
So go on then,
what are you waiting for?

Stan, you won't believe what these are made out of!

Flour, bits of pig, snout, ears, and lard.
Water, interesting intestines, and lard.
Added additives, preserving preservatives, and lard.
Glue, gristle and gelatinous gloop all made from:

LARD.

YUCK!

I wonder what's so special about them? Let's try one out on Daz the bully.

The Plot Thickens and Begins to Bubble

I've brought a pie to school,
Am acting on a hunch.
Yes! Daz, the bully, nicks it:
'Ta, George, time for lunch!'

He wolfs it down . . . how odd,
His sneer has disappeared.
'These pies are dead amazing,'
Says Daz, who's gone all weird.

Instead of pinching my arm
Or crushing my toes in a vice,
As we rush out for break
He does his best to be nice!

'Your will is my command,'
He says with a robot's tone,
His eyes are all glazed over,
It's just me and him alone.

This must be a stupid joke . . .
Say, 'I'm a currant bun!'
He does as I command:
I've never had so much fun!

These pies are something special,
And I'm really quite surprised,
For Daz the bully boy
Is totally **hypnotized**.

Daz even laughs at my awful jokes!

Annoying James Bond Jokes

What do you call the Spy Who Came In From the Cold?
Licensed to chill.

What do you call the spy who interrogated a beef burger?
Licensed to grill.

What do you call a spy disguised as a budgie?
Licensed to trill.

Oh, you're the funny one . . . what a laugh . . . you should be a comedi- an . . . you should get your own TV show . . . oh stop it now, my stom- ach can't take it any more . . .

What do you call a
spy who doubles as
a dentist?
Licensed to drill.

What do you call
a spy who doubles
as a dentist, later
that day?
Licensed to fill.

How does a spy
like his milkshake?
Shaken, but not stirred.

What do you call a
spy who came sec-
ond in the race?
Shaken but not third.

What time
does a spy eat
his breakfast?
007.

Snap Out of It!

Time to stop this. Now let's see.
Snap my fingers, count to three.
Has it worked? I think it has,
As Robot turns back into Daz!

George's List of Things to Do

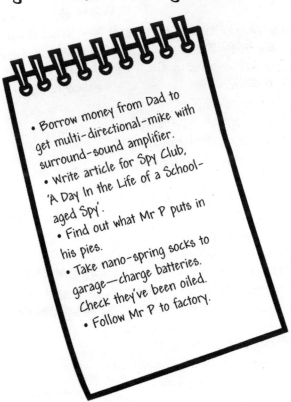

- Borrow money from Dad to get multi-directional-mike with surround-sound amplifier.
- Write article for Spy Club, 'A Day In the Life of a School-aged Spy'.
- Find out what Mr P puts in his pies.
- Take nano-spring socks to garage—charge batteries. Check they've been oiled.
- Follow Mr P to factory.

I needed to decided if Mr Panz was cook or crook. Time to put on my nano-spring socks.

Coiled and ready

Spring into action

Sock it to 'em

(Might cause a **stink**)

Tailing the suspect in my very own private **Boinnng** 747

How to Be Invisible

You are the king of the Not-theres,
The shadow's best mate.
You have passed exams in skulking
And learnt how to
Wallpaper backgrounds,
Slip sideways through impossibility,
And be taken (if needs be) for a tree.
You are the sheik of short-cuts.
Your every breath melts into the air,
Your hair is a fetching shade of transparency,
And your clothes are so unnoticeable, no one notices
    anything.
You are so still
That migrating swallows will swoop down to stop
On top of your head for a breather.
When you pass by, it's like a cloud passing the sun.
One blink of an eye and you've gone:
Invisible, a ghost, you now qualify
To hide and seek through the streets and spy.

I needed to check out the Panz's Perfect Porky Pie Factory. Luckily, I have been breaking and entering since I was a toddler.

Break-in at the Meat Pie Factory

Suction pads for hands
Slither up the wall
Instant trampoline
To break my fall.

A skeleton key for the door,
I hear the wind give a moan,
And now the keypad alarm . . .
Oh dear, I'm on my own.

Think! I've only got seconds
As time now horribly flies.
With sudden inspiration
I type the letters of H-Y-P-N-O-T-I-Z-E.

I pad on rubber shoes
Then hear a whispering sound
There inside the office,
Three figures are gathered round.

I wish I had my Extra Ear,
As the only words I got
Were 'PM . . . **Parliament** . . . and **Power** . . .'
They were devising a cunning plot!

So intent on listening hard,
I step on a squeaky tread.
The conversation stops
And my heart is filled with dread.

I run like the shadow of a jet,
Pausing only to pick up a sheet
That has some words hidden on it
In a code that is very discreet.

I took the piece of paper with me to school and hid in the loo to try and decipher it. Can you decipher it as well?

The Secret Code

```
        S F G E W Q X R E M E M B E R
      X Z L H J R E M E M B E R F P R
      T H E K Y Z X C V F I F T H J K Y
      E R O F S A X N O V E M B E R J
      X L S P E Z A T X V N M T H E L
      H P A R T Y F D S A J Y K T H E
      L P R I M E X A M I N I S T E R
      G B C E W I L L D F G H A V E O
      I U T Y A S U R P R I S E K J N L
      T X C D B A Q Z E A T I N G D F
      G E W Q T H O S E K G S D C X
      E W Y U M M Y Z U Y I H J R X Z
      H Y P N O T I C D B L R F G X L
      B P O R K M S V W T R P I E S W
```

Answer on page 126!

I had deciphered the code. The fifth of November was Guy Fawkes Night. What did it all mean? Then I saw the newspaper headline:

PANZ'S PERFECT PORKY PIES PARLIAMENT PARTY ON FIFTH OF NOVEMBER, CELEBRATING THE BEST OF BRITISH COOKERY.

Time to get home and write up my case notes, but then...

Rumbled!

'What are you up to?
Where have you been?
This bit of paper?
What does it mean?'

They've gone through my room!
How low can they stoop?
Only qualified spies
Are licensed to snoop!

But I've done my training,
And George shall be brave.
The truth will stay hidden
As a ghost in the grave!

Top Secret Weather Report (Decoded)

Today,
The sky was undercover
And the weather was definitely up to no good.
Raindrops tapped out their secret codes on rooftops,
And finally managed to infiltrate puddles.

Today,
The sun was in disguise,
No one would recognize her
In those nondescript baggy clothes.
Our organization on the ground
Began to doubt
If she ever even existed.

Today,
The clouds were on guard duty,
Walkie-talkies blaring thunder
With wheeling crows for sunglasses.

Today,
Autumn was betrayed
And the trees were shaking with fear.
The ground was sprinkled with leaf-codes
And the wind rifled through the endless golden piles
Trying to work out what they meant.

Today,
Bonfires sent out secret smoke signals,
Roasted chestnuts were too hot to handle
And soon, if all went according to plan,
There would be
Fireworks.

I had to warn the Prime Minister! Time for a disguise!

Instant Adult Kit

Telescopic legs
Computerized voice-deepener.
Instant beard cream.
Shaggy eyebrow-developer.
Wrinkle-cutter.
Worry-line pencil.
Glue-on armpit hair.
Pre-prepared adult conversation cards
(Guaranteed to be boring, e.g.:
'Strange weather for the time of year. What ho!')
And a free extra strap-on beer belly
(With rechargeable built-in wobble).

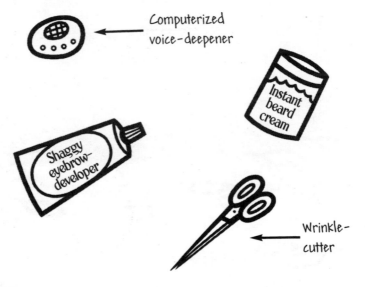

Computerized
voice-deepener

Instant
beard
cream

Shaggy
eyebrow-
developer

Wrinkle-
cutter

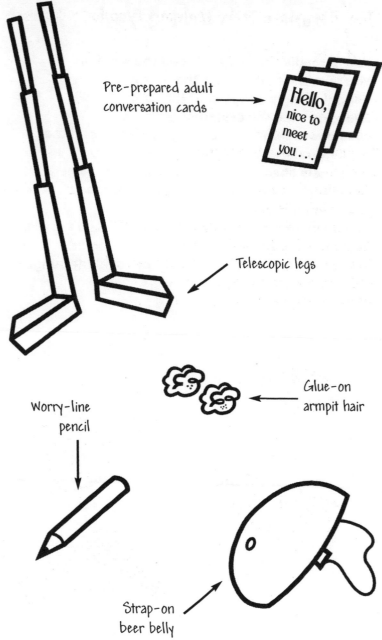

Pre-prepared adult conversation cards

Hello, nice to meet you . . .

Telescopic legs

Glue-on armpit hair

Worry-line pencil

Strap-on beer belly

107

Big Brother is Watching You!

'You're totally transparent!' said the window.
'You're in the frame!' said the mirror.
'Careful, I might snap!' said the camera.
'Eye! Eye!' said the captain.
'Eyes down! Two fat spies—eighty-eight!' said the
    bingo caller.
'I'm streets ahead of you!' said the CCTV camera.
'I'll brrring . . . brrring . . . bring you into focus!' said the
    cameraphone.
'You're making a spectacle of yourself!' said the glasses.
'What are you goggling at?' said the goggles.
'There's something shady going on!' said the sunglasses.

Just popping out to Stan's firework party!
See you later!

More Spy-ku

The trees have lost their
disguise. But I have fooled my
nosy family.

Hidden in the back,
his van is white as snow, but
His purpose is black.

At Parliament – a Playscript

George: (Aside) **All these famous people. I'd love to get autographs, but my job is to be part of the furniture.**

Butlers enter, stage left, bearing silver salvers piled with pies. Politicians drool noisily. Sounds of tummies rumbling. Prime Minister reaches hand towards pie and is about to bite.

George: (interrupting—with beard falling off)
Mr Prime Minister, Don't eat the pie.
It's dangerous! I'll explain why . . .

Mr Panz moves across stage towards action as if greased by butter.

Mr Panz: Sir, this unexpected and unpleasant surprise
is a bunch of boyish, made-up lies!
Please do carry on, there is nothing to fear,
My porky pies are in the clear!
(In one smooth action lifts unmodified pie from pocket to mouth so that PM cannot see.)
Look, I'll have a little bite!
See, I'm fine, in fact I'm totally all right!

(Shoves tray of hypnotic pies politely in PM's face.)

George: (shouting now)
Those pies are hypnotic! Eat them? Do not!
Your friend and deputy is part of the plot.
(Look of shock on Deputy PM's face)

Deputy PM: (To PM)
Dear friend, don't believe it, we've always been pally,
And this boy is bonkers, he must be doolally!
Now excuse me for a moment if you will,
There's a little something that I need to (aside to audience)

KILL!

George exits stage left pursued by Deputy PM, Panz, and various security officers. For the moment, the pies remain uneaten.

The Chase

It's no good, I've lost the day, time for me to slip away.
Out of the door into the street, hear the sound of
   following feet.
On my board I zip outside, but where to go and where
   to hide?
Leaping steps I am on track, but, oh, what's this?
   A cul-de-sac!

Trapped!

Deputy PM:
I'm sick of the futility,
Of being a mere Deputy.
Yes, it will improve my mood,
When the PM eats this food.
Such experiments we tried:
Pies genetically modified.
We worked in secret on ideas
Developed slowly through the years.
What is it that will help me rule?
My hypnotic molecule!
Once added to a tasty dish,
Then all will do just as I wish!
So say goodbye Democracy!
I'll take my place in history!
So come, dear George, your turn to try
A morsel of my home-made pie.
Once eaten, there will be no fear
As you simply disappear!

George: (aside)
This guy's pies might be hypnotic,
Their creator? He's psychotic!

Then suddenly from nowhere came a bit of help!

It's a Family Affair

Mum: A gun that shoots toffee
Could be a bit tricky,
His end isn't sweet
But somewhat sticky!

Dad: Press the button,
Liquid crash
Mini water-cannon
Makes a good splash.

Uncle Q: As a gadget this biro
Should win an award!
It proves that the pen
Is mightier than the sword.

Sister: Tennis ball machine-gun,
He's so easy to despatch,
Pummelled to the ground—
Game, set, and match!

George: In the end,
It's what saved me:
A bunch of spies—
My family!

The News at Breakfast!

PORKY PIES PERIL!
At the party, the Prime Minister uncovered a dreadful plot.

HYPNOSIS HORROR HEADED OFF!
The whole government was nearly taken over by power-mad deputy PM, Mr William Annabee along with his accomplice, former school cook, Mr Panz.

BEATEN BY A BOY!
Local boy, George Goldfinger uncovered the plot and confronted W. Annabee but nearly ended up hypnotized under Panz. Luckily, his family came to the rescue.

NEARLY NIGHT-KNIGHT
Having nearly lost his life in the service of his country, George

Goldfinger is youngest ever person to be knighted.

PANZ PRISON PUNISHMENT
Mr Panz and W. Annabee have both been sentenced to life imprisonment. George Goldfinger has been offered his own TV series and a million-pound book deal.

Secret Agent Sustenance

Beans on camouflaged toast,
Sly sausages,
Eggs that are not what they seem,
Tortured cabbage,
A dab of undercover ketchup,
Washed down with
Truth-telling tea.

Of course I never handed in the other pies to the police, but kept them in my freezer. They come in very useful!

Daz, the Bully, and Me

Thanks to Daz, life at school
Is no longer harsh and cruel.
No idea, what to do,
When homework's piling up on you?
The solution simply is that I
Offer Daz a porky pie.
Then he'll do my will, what's more—
He even opens every door.
With this spell, he's under my thumb,
Daz the bully's now a chum!

The Spy Rap

The name is George, that's right, that's me,
Chillin' at home with my family.
We're the superspies, yeah, we don't like lies,
Our powers of detection will hyp-no-tize!
Uncle Q is the man on the scene
With gadgets galore, he's a mean machine!
From nano-spring socks to the Barbie-doll tracker
And a tennis ball machine-gun that will take out
   that attacker.
I might look small, but we ain't small fry
Take us on? You don't even wanna try,
Cos I'm the grandmaster of this game,
Super-Snooper is my middle name.
We're the superspies, we're the undercover crew,
Baddies beware, cos we're gonna get you!

A Final Word

The world has now been saved
And it's time for me to fly.
This book will shortly self-destruct
So close it quick! Goodbye!

Index of Titles and First Lines

(First lines are in **bold**)

Answers

p. 60 I'm Going Crackers, Cracking Codes!:

1. Hello
2. Mirror, mirror, on the wall,
Who is the cleverest of them all?
3. I came, I saw, I conquered the code!

p. 65 Work Out the Code: there are no right answers—it doesn't make any sense!

p. 90 Another Riddle: follow

p. 102 The Secret Code:

Remember, remember, the fifth of November
At the party, the Prime Minister will have a surprise
Eating those yummy, hypnotic pork pies.

About Andrew Fusek Peters

Andrew Fusek Peters is a poet, author, storyteller, broadcaster, and didgeridoo player, and has written and edited more than forty-five children's titles, including **Ghosts Unlimited** and **Spies Unlimited** for Oxford University Press.

His acclaimed poetry collection **Poems With Attitude** and his verse novel **Crash!** (both with Polly Peters) were longlisted for the Carnegie Medal. His poems have appeared on **Poetry Please, Blue Peter** and the BBC1 poetry series **Wham Bam, Strawberry Jam**, and have been recorded online and on CD for the Poetry Archive, set up by the poet laureate—for more information, visit www.poetryarchive.org.

Andrew lives with his wife Polly and their two children in a converted old chapel in Shropshire.

More details are available on Andrew's books by visiting www.tallpoet.com.

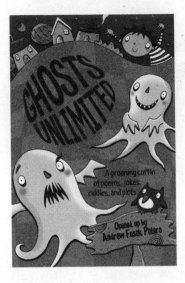

Fred can't get enough of ghosts—he's obsessed!—but in the graveyard is a secret entrance to a place where he can have more fun than he ever imagined. Barry the Bully had better watch out . . .

Ghoulish jokes, funky rhymes, shadowy riddles and a sizzling plot—all from dynamic poet, writer, and broadcaster Andrew Fusek Peters.

ISBN-13: 978-0-19-276330-3
ISBN-10: 0-19-276330-X

Illustrations by Nathan Reed